Feelings of a Girl

Val McFadden

BookLeaf Publishing

Presentation by *BookLeaf Publishing*

Web: www.bookleafpub.com

E-mail: info@bookleafpub.com

ISBN: 9789395950138

First edition 2022

DEDICATION

I dedicate this book to Brian, Jacob and Thomas

ACKNOWLEDGEMENT

I am grateful and thankful to my husband, Brian and my two boys for their unconditional love and support.

True

Lovely, caring, honest and True
That's what family means to you
You say these words with true conviction
But your actions show such contradiction

My brain is tired from trying to think
To work it out, I'm on the brink
Caring and kindness, I know I deserve
However my sanity I must preserve

I wish it was different every day
If only I could have a say
My voice is quiet to your delight
To hear my voice would be to fight

But what if, my quiet was my power
That I could grow just like a flower
With nurture and love, with care too
The people who can share my brew

I decided quiet was right for me
So I can be loved unconditionally
This is what will guide me through
Even though I look like I withdrew

Fresh

Summer sun
Warm and delicious
On your face
Fresh

Doggy licks
Wet and slobbery
On your legs
Fresh

Beach bum
Sandy and glorious
On your toes
Fresh

Grassy haven
Green and tickly
On your fingers
Fresh

Children playing
Loud and joyful
In your ears

Fresh

Burgers cooking
Tempting and tasty
In your mouth
Fresh

Against your skin
In your senses
All is summer and all is fresh
To me and breathe

Fine

What a word Fine can be
"I'm fine." Is said so we can see
To hide away what lie's beneath
Sometimes said through gritted teeth

Fine can be for very good
That's a fine carved piece of wood
A joy for everyone to behold
To admire or even touched with gold

It can be an exceptionally fine line
Like silk or thread or even twine
Drawn thinly on the paper shown
Or thread to make a picture sewn

Unlucky enough to receive a fine
Especially if you've been a swine
A payment made for speeding maybe
Not paying attention and being lazy

Fine can also mean satisfactory
All is okay in my world actually

Who would have thought one simple word
Could mean so much, how absurd!
"It's fine!"

Course

It's time to visit college again
To learn about counselling
A group of us that we will cherish
Spending time that we will relish

Listening with empathy
And not offering sympathy
Loving unconditionally
And making it traditionally

Sadness

Sometimes it can consume me
Knowing what I've lost
You'll never hear my plea
You'll never know the cost

My sadness radiates out
Spreading for all to see
It tells everyone that I'm without
One day I hope to be free

Dad

The hardest poem to write of all
Is this one, a block just like a wall
I had two Dad's whilst growing tall
Dad and real Dad, their names I'd call

My biological is plain to see
It's just not that easy for me to be
My stepdad is my Dad to me
The Dad who kissed my grazed knee

My biological wanted his daughter more
To be there when he needs her, sure
This shook me to my core
My wounded feelings are very sore

My Dad was the one who was kind
Was patient with me and didn't mind
When I played up and was a bind
With hide and seek, he'd come and find

Now Dad is gone away to cancer
I miss him every day, my lancer
With limited mobility, he wasn't a dancer
One day let's hope we have an answer

Annoying

Annoying, frustrating and a bit pissed off
When annoyance kicks in, it starts like a
bomb
It feels like it's never ending, but it ends in a
flash
It's super annoying, but not any bad

It's usually when you don't get your own
way
But feeling angry is always okay
Sometimes it's painful or hurting your heart
It can be verbal and tear you apart
It feels different from person to person
As people are different,
and nobody can be the same

Holiday

Excitement building, getting ready to set
The children, "Are we nearly there yet."
Hustle and bustle, can we fit everything in
A child is shouting, oh what a din

We've arrived, our place is spick and span
And time to unpack, whatever we can
We head to the beach, lovely sea air
This is the place, that's without a care

Cornwall

Sand and water against your toes
Here is a place that anything goes
A waterfall flows through the rock
A way away a babbling brook

A castle high up on the hill
Where King Arthur sat so still
Wild fields upon the moors
So many beautiful places to lure

Little islands visable from shore
Can see why we come back for more
A theatre carved into the rock
Time and again, we come to look

Tales of smuggling from long ago
Some looting which is all they know
The sea is so clear, sparkling and blue
No better place for me, that's true

Hilly walks and rocky paths
Way down can see the lifeguard flags

A boat ride, way out to sea
The Cornish coast as it should be

Today

Today we walked for several miles
Up and down hills, and finding coves
Walking along produced many smiles
Looking down at the many cloves

Walking in the sunshine bright
Watching the rowers racing along
The whole scene brings such delight
I feel this is where I belong

Relaxing in this Cornish world
A pastie to ease our hunger pangs
Waves crashing as the sea swirled
Sand is falling from our hands

Solitude

We found a beach call Lanivet
It was so quiet and private
The tide was high when we arrived
A place where we didn't feel deprived

The tide was starting its big reveal
Little by little, looking majestically ideal
Round the corner a bit more sand
Just watching the beach slowly expand

A little cave has become visible
Nature showing how hospitable
She can be if you watch and wait
Let Nature be and she will create

A few hours later can walk across
The rocks whilst they show who's boss
The waves thrash and crash so high
As if they were trying to hit the sky

Over the rocks we can climb now
The solitude is absolutely wow
The other side a full empty beach
That was just before out of reach

Children

The awe when our baby is born
Those bright eyes looking for everything
Burrowed brows sometimes with scorn
As parents we will keep carrying

Then a toddler stands up tall
An easily overwhelmed little boy
Who can think that one so small
With oodles of love to enjoy

And off to school they soon go
Loving learning and gaining power
Going to go with the flow
And growing just like a flower

Before you know it's exams and tests
To see what works, the key to being
At long as you can do your best
Choose something for your well-being

Bickering

Oh how I love my children so
However the bickering can make me go
A little crazy, back and forth
Sometimes I wish I could send them north

He said I couldn't play just now
I wish I could just understand how
He won't let me join his game
Another day, it's just the same

He took the remote off me
He's on his phone when he shouldn't be
He's not eating his dinner up
He's split my drink from my cup

On and on it continues to
Who's right or wrong, what is true
My wish for them to get along
And one day sing the same song

Anniversary

Hello to our anniversary
For 17 years we've been wed today
Our love has grown along the way
As we celebrate this special day
With cards to express what we say
One day we hope to go away
A remote coastal destination stay
One day even via Calais
We continue on and hope and pray
To keep our love, honour and obey
We make sure we still can play
Maybe one day we'll learn crochet
To ensure our love does not sway
By sticking together we will be okay

Lola

Puss cat, oh puss cat
Curled up on my lap
Purring away with contentment
You act so independent

Your tabby stripey fur
Soft and shiny while you purr
A happy cat at that
Even when you chase a rat

Doggy

Sunshine and shaggy hair
Running like you don't care
Looking like a little bear
You are beautiful and rare

You chase after the ball
Coming back when we call
Occasionally you may fall
Legs akimbo in the hall

Bum wagging in happiness
You show how to express
Your doggy smiling gladness
With a great success

The beach is your favourite place
Chasing pebbles with good grace
Your moustache on your doggy face
Wet with sea, it looks ace

Best of all is your cuddles
Takes away all my troubles
Sometimes wet after puddles
But still the best for huddles

Loud

The loudness hurts my ears
Sometimes I feel the tears
It expands my fears
I hide until it clears
Or what makes the sound appears
Or the sound disappears
And no longer hurts my ears

Flowers

Flowers bloom with petals galore
Colours blossoming showing their beauty
Sharing their perfume with the air
Showing love to all who notice

Pinks and whites, yellow and reds
From blooming buds is natures glory
Unfolding to reveal beautiful heads
Alive for a while, until petals fall

Feelings

So many feelings within us
Sometimes we may feel disgust
Repelled and horrible and hesistant
Not feeling any merriment

Sometimes anxious and overwhelmed
Worried, fearful and expelled
Inferior, weak and inadequate
Left feeling dispassionate

At times humiliated and bitter
Wanting to be a quitter
Also can feel betrayed and furious
And a little bit curious

Sometimes busy, stressed and rushed
Life can feel very pressured
Along with feeling tired and sleepy
Which can also feel quite weepy

We can also feel astonished and amazed
Hoping we get lots of praise
Excited, eager and energetic
Making sure we're not apologetic

Other times feeling content and free
I guess you wouldn't disagree
Curious, interested and inquisitive
Whilst showing lots of initiative

Feeling loving, peaceful and thankful
Life can feel so tranquil
When we're valued and accepted
Respected and protected